Holidays and Celebrations

Thanksgiving

by Brenda Haugen
illustrated by Todd Ouren

Thanks to our advisers for their expertise, research, and advice:

Alexa Sandmann, Ed.D., Professor of Literacy
The University of Toledo, Toledo, Ohio
Member, National Council for the Social Studies

Susan Kesselring, M.A., Literacy Educator
Rosemount-Apple Valley-Eagan (Minnesota) School District

PICTURE WINDOW BOOKS
MINNEAPOLIS, MINNESOTA

For Grandma Bernie, whom I give thanks for every day

Managing Editor: Bob Temple
Creative Director: Terri Foley
Editor: Sara E. Hoffmann
Editorial Adviser: Andrea Cascardi
Copy Editor: Laurie Kahn
Designer: Melissa Voda
Page production: The Design Lab
The illustrations in this book were rendered digitally.

Picture Window Books
5115 Excelsior Boulevard
Suite 232
Minneapolis, MN 55416
1-877-845-8392
www.picturewindowbooks.com

Printed in the United States of America.

Library of Congress Cataloging-in-Publication Data
Haugen, Brenda.
Thanksgiving / by Brenda Haugen ; illustrated by Todd Ouren.
p. cm. — (Holidays and celebrations)
Summary: Briefly discusses the history and customs connected to the celebration
of Thanksgiving in the United States.
Includes bibliographical references.
ISBN 1-4048-0191-X
1. Thanksgiving Day—Juvenile literature. [1. Thanksgiving Day. 2. Holidays.]
I. Ouren, Todd, ill. II. Title. III. Holidays and celebrations (Picture Window Books)
GT4975 .H38 2004
394.2649—dc21
                                                                    2003006102

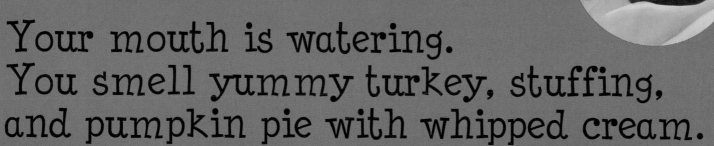

Your mouth is watering.
You smell yummy turkey, stuffing,
and pumpkin pie with whipped cream.

It's Thanksgiving!
Do you know how this holiday started?

Almost 400 years ago, the Pilgrims left England to come to America. They sailed on a ship called the *Mayflower.*

The Pilgrims left England because they wanted to be able to choose their own church. They did not have that choice in England.

When the Pilgrims sailed to America, they landed in Plymouth, Massachusetts.

The Pilgrims' lives in America were hard.
They did not know how to plant crops.
They did not know how to hunt.

When winter came, the Pilgrims were very cold. They did not know how to build warm houses.

About half the Pilgrims died that first winter. They were cold and did not have enough food.

A kind Native American decided to help them. His name was Squanto.

Squanto taught the Pilgrims to hunt and fish.
He showed them how to plant vegetables.

Squanto used fish as fertilizer. Fertilizer makes the ground rich and helps plants grow.

In autumn, the Pilgrims harvested their crops. They had enough food for the cold winter to come.

They were thankful for Squanto's help.
They invited Squanto and his friends
to a huge feast.

They ate clams, eel, and other fish from the ocean. They ate pumpkin, dried fruits, and corn they had grown.

They played games. They also gave thanks for all they had.

Some families still play games on Thanksgiving. Some watch football games on television.

15

Today, people still give thanks. They still have feasts, but some of the food is a little different.

People eat turkey, stuffing, cranberries, and pumpkin pie.

The Pilgrims didn't have forks. They ate with spoons, knives, and their fingers!

Many people watch Thanksgiving parades. Some of these parades are shown on television.

The parades have marching bands, big balloons, and fancy floats. They are big celebrations!

Millions of people watch the Macy's Thanksgiving Day Parade every year. It is in New York City.

The first Thanksgiving
did not include fancy floats
and big parades. It started
with Squanto and the Pilgrims.
They gave us this special holiday,
which began as a harvest feast.

The Pilgrims' lives
were very hard, but
they still celebrated
what they had.

Thanksgiving is a time for family and friends.
It is a time for sharing and being grateful
for what we have.

You Can Make a Fall Leaf Rubbing

What you need:

  real leaf
  piece of paper
  crayons

What you do:

1. Put your leaf on a flat surface.
2. Cover the leaf with your sheet of paper.
3. Holding the paper in place, use the crayons to color on the paper over the leaf.
4. The leaf's image will appear on your sheet of paper!

Fun Facts

- A writer named Sarah Josepha Hale encouraged President Abraham Lincoln to create a national day of thanks. This is how Thanksgiving became a holiday.

- President Lincoln chose the date for Thanksgiving in the United States. He picked the last Thursday in November. Many years later, Congress chose the fourth Thursday in November as Thanksgiving Day.

- In Canada, Thanksgiving is the second Monday in October.

- The Pilgrims probably did not have any sweet foods at their harvest meal. To make sweet foods, you need sugar. The Pilgrims had little or no sugar at the time of their feast.

- In the 17th century, people did not use teaspoons and tablespoons for measuring ingredients. Instead, they guessed how much of each ingredient should go into the food!

Words to Know

Congress—the group of people who make the laws for the United States

crop—a plant grown in large amounts

feast—a big meal

fertilizer—a substance that makes the land richer and helps crops grow better

float—a decorated truck or flat platform that forms part of a parade

harvest—to pick and gather crops

To Learn More

At the Library

Anderson, Laurie Halse. **Thank You, Sarah!: The Woman Who Saved Thanksgiving**. New York: Simon & Schuster Books for Young Readers, 2002.

Corey, Shana. **Milly and the Macy's Parade**. New York: Scholastic Press, 2002.

Hayward, Linda. **The First Thanksgiving**. New York: Random House, 2003.

Hintz, Martin. **Thanksgiving: Why We Celebrate It the Way We Do**. Mankato, Minn.: Capstone Press, 1996.

Rau, Dana Meachen. **Thanksgiving**. New York: Children's Press, 2000.

Fact Hound

Fact Hound offers a safe, fun way to find Web sites related to this book. All of the sites on Fact Hound have been researched by our staff.
http://www.facthound.com

1. Visit the Fact Hound home page.
2. Enter a search word related to this book, or type in this special code: 140480191X.
3. Click on the FETCH IT button.

Your trusty Fact Hound will fetch the best sites for you!

Index

church, 6
crops, 8, 12
England, 6
feast, 12–13, 16–17, 20–21, 23
Mayflower, 6–7
parades, 18–19, 20
Pilgrims, 6–13, 17, 20, 23
Squanto, 10–11, 13, 20
winter, 9, 12